But God

The Story of a Life Used for His Glory

Sonya Michelle Snell

B.O.Y. Publications, Inc.
c/o Author Copyrights
P.O. Box 262
Lowell, NC 28098
betonyourselfent.com

Paperback ISBN: 978-1-955605-61-8

Cover and Interior Design: B.O.Y. Enterprises, Inc.

Printed in the United States.

Dedication

To my Lord and Savior Jesus Christ for being my forever rescue story! To my husband Ben, my confidant and the love of my life, who has walked every step of the meaningful moments with me every day. To my children Jermir, Shyia, Jordan, and Ephraim as well as my grandchildren Jade and Jayce, who continue to inspire me to share stories that matter.

Table of Contents

Introduction

The word *but* of the English language is communicated in and out of our conversations on a day-to-day basis. It means, "except, save, on the contrary, aside from". It is a small word but useful in enhancing the meaning of surrounding words and signaling appropriate pause. In this book, my desire is to passionately share with you, the reader, how meaningful, powerful, life changing and purposeful the words "But God" really are and how they signify a redirection in what we are able to accomplish according to the power and works of God.

The wordage "but God" appears verbatim as an imperative view/perception throughout the entirety of the Bible. But God...yield, go along with, sit still for God's power, sovereignty, and majesty. God's grace and love are incomparable and unmatched! Oh, He is everywhere, all-knowing, always. God our sovereign creator is also our loving good, good Father. The many names of God used in conjunction with "but" support and acknowledge who He is in contrast to our limited ability and knowledge, found from the first page of scripture on through the New Testament.

The world we live in is a wreck surrounded by chaos, confusion, sadness, sickness, hate, unforgiveness and the list could go on and on. The enemy runs wreckage. In certain circumstances, he appears to succeed. Many people suffer, and many succumb to his devices. I've come to tell you, even if you have found yourself in that number, the story is not over. God's plan is and has always been perfect. God's intent was to rescue us all along. But God!

To follow Christ is to gain an everlasting hope, and eternal life with God in Heaven. These two words, *but God* also tell us that we have been saved only by God's grace. I've had many, many *But God* moments that always remind me of His faithfulness and His goodness in my life.

This book is set apart to share MY story about MY life literally being MY testimony all the while giving God the glory and magnifying His name. I have sections throughout the book that are titled staying in the moment. As I looked back at my journey, I noticed there were moments that seemed normal at the time. These are moments we take for granted when really, we should be grateful and thankful for every moment even the small ones we view as common. Also, I have included moments to reflect, where I invite you, the reader, to reflect on your life.

My story is my testimony. My life is my testimony. Me having the ability to write this book is a direct reflection of a *But God* moment and being placed here for His glory. Come along with me as I share the goodness of God in my life. Prayerfully you will be encouraged, strengthened, and will leap for joy with me as I share the sovereignty of God in my blessed life!!

Moment 1

Tuesday, September 22, 2020, started out as what I thought was a "normal day". I had worked from home as the world was experiencing the COVID Pandemic. Meaning my workdays looked a lot different, as many others. I went on my daily prayer walk up and down my driveway, then cooked dinner as usual. My daughter had just graduated from college back in December and decided to come back home for a while. Our oldest son Jermiroquan was now married and out the house with his family, and the younger two sons Jordan and Jahnarious both were off in college. Ben, my husband, was working night shift on this day. So, it was just me and my daughter at home. We had dinner together. Afterward I prepared for bed, did some reading, then drifted off to sleep. I can remember my daughter coming into my room as she does every night to say good night and I love you. When she did, I woke up, gathered my materials, called it a night, and said my prayers. I went to sleep feeling absolutely fine, normal, nothing out of the ordinary,

Ben had worked until 3 AM that Wednesday September 23, 2020, and came home a little past 3 and I remember hearing him come in and me waking up to greet him as we've done for the past 20 something years, then turning back over and falling back to sleep. Again, nothing out of the ordinary. Though it was a normal routine of things, never would I have thought that a couple of hours later our lives would change forever.

Staying in the Moment: I'm grateful to have had the chance to exchange smiles, spend quality family time, embrace, kiss and say I love you; to have conversations with family throughout that day. That day's interaction, that quick moment spent with my husband at 3 in the morning could have been my last. We never know when it very well will be our last conversations, our last opportunity to be present, our last time physically on this earth. I was reminded as I spent time thinking about what God had done, of how vital moments, minutes and even seconds really are. Do not take life for granted. It may be cliché but, in all honesty, as much as I can impress upon you; make the most of the time you are given for yourself and the people you love. Remember to be intentional about making room for the things that really matter.

Moment of Reflection: Take a moment, reflect on your day. Tell someone you love them, be a help to yourself and others today. Use the space below to express your gratitude for today.

_____

_____

_____

_____

_____

_____

_____

_____

_____

_____

_____

_____

_____

_____

_____

_____

_____

_____

_____

_____

Moment 2

My husband proceeds to get himself ready for bed and got settled in. He crawls into bed next to me and falls to sleep as usual as we have done life together with shift work for over 23 years now. Nothing new here. Well as the morning progressed things changed quickly. My husband says he was awakened to me breathing very strangely and making a strange noise. Knowing this sounded different, he nudged me and thought nothing of it. He thought I would correct what sounded strange and he would go back to sleep. However, I did not respond. I continue to show signs that something was terribly wrong.

He nudged me again and called my name this time "Sonya"! Again, no response. He jumped out of bed, turned the light on all while calling my name, panicking. He walks over to me, shakes me, "Sonya, Sonya, Sonya!" Ben ran to the bathroom get some water and proceeded to throw water on my face, still no response from me. He also told me he literally slapped me a couple of times (I wonder how hard, hahaha.) in an attempt to wake me and get a response. He did all that to get me to respond to him, but I did not, not because I did not want to, but because I could not.

We have been married 26 years now and have an amazing relationship. We joked a lot but not this time, I was not joking around. He says he then called my mom over the phone to let her know what was happening, hung up from her and then called 911. All the while, I had no idea what was happening to me and all the commotion that was going on around me. I did not hear, feel, or remember anything during this entire time.

Staying in the Moment: I am not sure where I was or exactly what was going on with me naturally but spiritually, I am confident that I was resting safely in the arms of my Lord and Savior Jesus. I was covered and protected under His sovereignty. I am grateful for the nudge from God to my husband that let Ben know I needed attention. I am grateful for my husband's obedience, attentiveness, and love for me that did not let him rest but caused him to fight for me.

Moment of Reflection: Take a moment, remember a time in your life (even if it is right now) when you needed a connection to the power of God to reverse what could be or could've been. Write your experience below.

_____

_____

_____

_____

_____

_____

_____

_____

_____

_____

_____

_____

_____

_____

_____

_____

_____

_____

_____

_____

_____

_____

_____

Moment 3

After about 15 minutes of my husband going back and forth, I finally heard him and responded. Praise Jesus! I hold it to be true and I'm confident that the following things were the reasons I was able to pop up:

- The tears, prayers, and love from my husband towards me and for God,
- My personal relationship with the good, good Father
- God's love for me connected with my spirit which tapped into my soul.
- The power of the Holy Ghost and sovereignty of God touched and communicated to my body.

When all of those elements combined, I woke up in Jesus' Name! I know the Lord touched me with His finger of love and allowed me to respond. My response was delayed, but I responded. I sat up on the edge of our bed. I could remember feeling very confused initially because I could hear my husband's voice of panic. As I sat up, I was trying to figure out why he was calling my name in such urgency. What was going on?

Well, it didn't take very long for me to realize that something was terribly wrong and that the *something* causing alarm was with me. I sat up and uttered the words, "What's wrong bae?" and before he could respond to explain to me what happened, I immediately fell back onto the bed. I had no strength. I was having a pain in my head I have never felt before. I felt nauseous, extremely weak, and my vision was blurry. I had never felt this way ever in my life. I wasn't sure what I was experiencing but I knew within myself that it was serious.

I listened to my husband ask me questions I did not have the answers for, as I was trying my best to figure out what was going on as well. Everything so quickly, all the thoughts of concern, worry, and fear were filling my head. Like I was just fine. I've been fine, no health issues, no medications, I was healthy. Had just laid down for the night from a normal day, I was just fine. Yes, I didn't have the answers I could not answer any of the questions, nor did I have a clue as to what was going on, *but God!* I knew without a doubt who knew and who was there, and who would take good care of Sonya.

My daughter was upstairs still asleep for the night. Ben had not called or alerted her yet. Once I came to, he called for her. She was startled and wondered, why is dad yelling for me so loudly at this time in the morning? She too was confused. She came down and he told her your mom is sick come help me get her ready. We have to take her to the hospital. She came to me and stood by my side of the bed, looked me in my eyes and with concern said, "Ma what's wrong? I just talked to you, and you were fine." Again, I did not have an answer to that question. At this point the strength and power of God seemed to push me into a fight mode. No, I didn't know what was going on but I knew it wasn't good and it wasn't time to allow whatever was happening to just happen, so I needed to fight! So, I did all I could do and knew to do…I grabbed her around her waist and responded with tears in eyes and a call to the Father! "Shyia, Mommy don't know what is happening, but mommy don't want to be sick," and I started calling on the name of Jesus!

"Jesus, Jesus, Jesus!"

My mom had gotten in touch with my sister Shelia and around that time she called. I could hear her on the phone with Ben asking a series of questions and she then called out for me. "Sonya, what's going on? How are you feeling?" I began to tell her how I was feeling. In the middle of the conversation she said, "You will be ok." You see, she is a Nurse Practitioner and has been in medical field for 20 plus years. So, hearing us describe had taken place, I believe she was attempting to encourage everyone. But my immediate and bold response to her was, "I AM OK!" At that moment, I had shifted gears from fear and uncertainty to assurance and faith in the true and living God.

Staying in the Moment: No, I wasn't sure. Matter of fact, I had no idea what was going on with me but what I did know was that God was in control of it all. Nothing happens concerning me without His permission. I knew God was fighting for me and that He was with me. So yes, I was already OK. Yes, I was confused, scared, and very sick, but my spirit man was calm, encouraged, bold, and calling on the name of Jesus!

Moment of Reflection: Think of a time you didn't know what was going on and how things were going to turn out, but you knew God was in control. Write about your experience below.

_____

_____

_____

_____

_____

_____

_____

_____

_____

_____

_____

_____

_____

_____

_____

_____

_____

_____

_____

_____

_____

Moment 4

When I looked at my daughter and said, "Shyia, Mommy don't want to be sick," those words came from a place of pure honesty and humbleness to God. It was a cry for help and total surrender. I grabbed her around her waist and began calling on the name of Jesus!!

"Jesus, Jesus, Jesus!"

My husband and daughter dressed me as I had no strength of my own. My mom and the ambulance arrived at the same time. My mom told me she asked them to allow her to enter before them so she could lay eyes on me first. She shared how she prayed to God the whole trip to our home. She was asking Him to help me, reminding God that He made me and knows all about me. She asked Him to please let her find me OK when she arrived. I watched as they all entered our bedroom, as I was laying there perplexed. I saw the look of concern on my mom's face and the sound of worry in her voice. She was trying her best to keep it together, but I could also tell she was praying.

As they entered our bedroom, my mom gently said, "Sonya are you ok? What's going on? It's going to be ok." The medical people began to ask me what I was experiencing. We began to have conversations about what had taken place. I proceeded to verbalize that I did not want them to take me to the hospital. My husband immediately responded to me, "You may not want to go with them," because he knew exactly what I was saying without me literally saying it, "but you are going to the hospital. Do you realize I could not wake you up? Something isn't right and we are not waiting or ignoring it. Let them take your vitals and if they check out fine, I am going to take you to the hospital." Praise God, my vitals all checked just fine. God was in the details!

My husband said, "OK let's get you in the car and I will take you to the ER." The ambulance left, my husband and mom basically carried me to the car, as I was too weak and sick to walk myself. My husband drove, my daughter sat on the passenger side upfront, and my mom sat in the back with me. As I laid my head in my mom's lap all I could do was pray and call on Jesus. It was Jesus and me walking through this thing! As I felt the concerns and prayers of those surrounding me, I knew I was covered!

Staying in the Moment: I was really sick and could barely move or sit up. I was weak beyond anything I'd ever felt, *but God*! When I tell you He gave me very present help, He did! The Lord, and oh I thank Him so much, allowed me to be in my right mind and gave me the strength to express to my husband my desires in the midst of a crisis. God is so good!! God spoke and nudged me. I was sick, but I was listening and knew He was in the details and midst. I told my husband I did not want to be taken by ambulance to the local hospital. For I knew that would mean being taken to a facility that was not in my best interest nor that I wanted to be. At the time I just knew what I knew from past experiences but as I had time to process, I realized how important it is to be intentional about where you are placed. Where you allow yourself to be placed can make a huge difference in the outcome of your situation. Following the direction of God even when you are desperate, pushed, or sick unto death is vital. Being in the right place is key.

Your environment and the bodies that surround you are vital. You need them to step up and step in and fight for you when you are too weak and can't fight for yourself. You need the love and care that is strong, firm, and built on the love of God and His power. My husband, oh the Lord blessed him so good, was graced to operate in husband mode, father mode, but mostly as the spiritual head of our home. So many emotions he dealt with unexpectedly and simultaneously, but the Lord was his help and he fought for me in more ways and so many levels without hesitation! How grateful I am! He knew where our help had come from and was going to come from. I am so glad he didn't give up on me, our family, our home, our seeds, our God, but instead he stood in the gap. Others as well went to God on my behalf including all of our kids, our immediate family, and our church family. They all got word and went into prayer. Thank you, Jesus. God turned it around and I thank Him for hearing our prayers and sparing my life and the hearts of my family.

Moment of Reflection: Take a moment to go over your circle, making sure your circle is solid and filled with God ordained individuals that are able and willing to go to war with you and for you when it really counts. Ensure your relationship with the Father is in the right standing so when you call on Him, He will answer by fire. Make a list of those in your circle who are willing and able to fight for you in prayer.

_____

_____

_____

_____

_____

_____

_____

_____

_____

_____

_____

_____

_____

_____

_____

_____

_____

_____

_____

Moment 5

It was in these moments that I knew God was in the details. The details of the timing of my sickness, the details of the decisions of the hospital I was taken to, resulting in my place of treatment for my diagnosis. I am sure had I been taken any other place; things would've been different. However, that morning God was in the details as He always is. He was right there fighting for me, and He worked all things together for my good, placing me for His glory!

When we arrived at the hospital, my husband pulled in the front and walked into the ER to communicate what was going on. He came back out with a wheelchair, got me out of the car and rolled me inside. They of course checked me in and immediately started running the test as well as performing a CT scan.

As I was lying in that hospital bed going in and out of sleep. The Lord allowed me to be calm in my spirit and mind, resting in Him. If you know me, that is a miracle all by itself. I have always had this thing with hospitals. I've never been comfortable going, would avoid it at all costs, and did not enjoy it a bit if the need to go was there. I didn't like anything about the hospital and my anxiety would be on 100 if I even needed to go for a visit. So, I know it to be true that Jesus makes the difference and that He truly is a mind regulator, heart fixer, and a peace that surpasses all understanding.

I didn't know what had happened, was happening and what was going to happen, but I remained calm, peaceful, restful, positive, unbothered, and firm in Jesus' name. And I give God the glory because I knew it was and continues to be nobody but Jesus. I began to say I shall live and not die. Repeatedly! I replaced the unknown with the known with the blessed assurance of Jesus. As I went to have tests and scans done, I was in prayer, encouraging myself and resting in the Lord.

We waited in that hospital ER room for whatever test results they had run. As we waited, different doctors and nurses began to come in and out of the room, as a team, checking on me, asking questions about how I was feeling. They asked questions that should be familiar to me, personal questions like what's your name, birthday etc. Then a team of doctors came in and began sharing with my husband and I that upon reviewing scan they saw bleeding on my brain.

OK! Those words, those findings were the furthest from my mind of what was happening. They proceeded with the fact that they would need to transfer me to MUSC for further evaluation and treatment because they didn't have the proper equipment. They communicated they had already called ahead, and the Neurology team was preparing for my arrival.

I could tell even though they saw what they saw in the test results, it wasn't matching what they were seeing in me per my actions. I was calm, aware, and responsive, because I was living in a *But God* moment!

Staying in the Moment: God is always in control fighting for us. He goes before us and fights for us. He had all the details all worked out. When my sister, the Nurse Practitioner, heard the diagnosis, she said, "But she's talking, she's aware, she's responding, she couldn't have had a brain aneurysm!" The medical community was amazed but my God is sovereign!

Moment of Reflection: List a time you knew/saw the sovereignty of God.

_____

_____

_____

_____

_____

_____

_____

_____

_____

_____

_____

_____

_____

_____

_____

_____

_____

_____

_____

_____

Moment 6

I was transported to MUSC by ambulance and my husband followed in our vehicle. I arrived at MUSC to a room full of medical staff awaiting me. They were prepared and were talking and moving fast. I was in this cold room with machines beeping and a lot of movement. They all were very compassionate. I could remember, the staff assuring me everything would be ok and that they would take great care of me. Things were moving so fast; I remember saying, "Hold up! Wait, let me call my husband before anything is done to me."

I had my cell phone and the last thing I remember from that arrival was me calling my husband and seeing where he was because they were moving fast. I hung up the phone saying I love you and that is all I remember. When I woke up later that afternoon, I had already had the surgery. I woke up and my husband was right by my side. I said, "Bae, what happened?" He told me I was diagnosed with and survived a Brain Aneurysm. I already had the surgery and now I would stay in the hospital for the next 14 days in recovery.

God's sovereignty is like no other!

I am the founder and visionary of Women of God on the Frontline a ministry that was birthed by God to serve, encourage, and empower women from all over. This women's ministry included hosting anointed, very impactful annual conferences. When the pandemic hit, Women of God on the Frontline shifted to virtual conferences. iCare iShare with Sonya and Friends LIVE segments via Facebook Live was birthed as an extension of WOGOTFL. It was placed on my heart to connect friends and sisters on the social media platform to share our victories and struggles as we were facing a time in all our lives that was different and difficult. God has gifted me with a heart for women, which drives my passion to empower and encourage!

Months leading up to my becoming sick, I was planning and had scheduled an iCare iShare with Sonya and Friends segment. It would be entitled, "The Sovereignty of God! Isaiah 43:1-7 "My portion does not result in the short end of the stick; it is the pathway to something greater!" It was scheduled to air that Friday evening September 25, 2020. I was hospitalized on Wednesday morning, September 23, 2020. I knew this was going to be a life changing inspirational segment because:

1. It came from the Lord. I always hear from Him on what to share, what is needed, what is helpful, and what is useful right now.
2. It had truth, every word held truth.
3. I believed what it was declaring.
4. The speakers I absolutely adore and knew their stories would be impactful to someone's life to meet them where they were.

So, I had been preparing and anticipating as usual. Then bam it happened, the theme for this segment took presence immediately in MY life! Here I am laying in that hospital bed after experiencing a life changing health scare, had gone through surgery for the brain aneurysm, and where I would spend the next 14 days. I would receive multiple blood transfusions, series of test, medications, IV hook ups, and bruised arms from massive needle sticks daily.

But God!

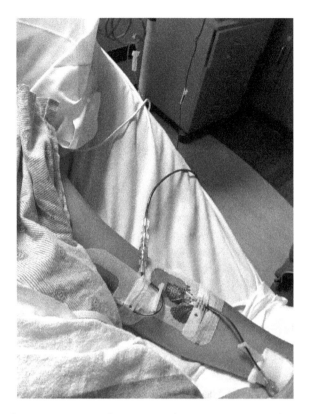

By the grace, goodness, and sovereignty of God at work in My Life, He allowed me to air the segment via FB Live with my friends from that hospital bed! Oh God, I thank you! God gave me enough strength to call each of them to explain what had taken place in a very short time. Of course, they were in awe that I was able to function the way I was and that I had the mind to still want to do the segment. We all gave God all the praise for what He had done in my life and oh man were we ready more than ever to bring this segment to fruition so all would get to witness the goodness of God!

I spent 14 days at The Medical University on the Neurology 9th floor under the care of Dr. Lena and his staff of doctors and the wonderful nurses I called my angels. Those 14 days were filled with blood drawing, daily medications, brain scans, daily neurology tests that consisted of questions and coordination of my movements. Every day I was there, the staff, as they rotated and made their rounds, were all so loving, caring, pleasant, available, accountable, and helpful. God blessed me the care of first class because that's what He does for His children!

Every day, every hour, every minute, every second, every moment was a miracle that I had lived to be a part of and witness. Every progress was a blessing, and I spent those days in a place of gratefulness! It was a process! Many of those days

I was in pain, exhausted from all the needle sticking, being waken up every hour, *but God*! The physical man was struggling but the spiritual man was encouraged! I knew in my heart that trouble don't last always and that this shall pass. If God brought me to it, He would surely bring me through it! I was surrounded by positive, Holy Ghost filled, family who loved me and loved God. They prayed with me and were there to support and help in any way that was needed. And I do mean any way. My husband tenderly cared for me in every way he could. From doing my hair to just being by my side in that hospital room every night on that hospital floor, on his blow-up mattress he went and purchased. He was not leaving my side. For that I am so grateful and blessed!

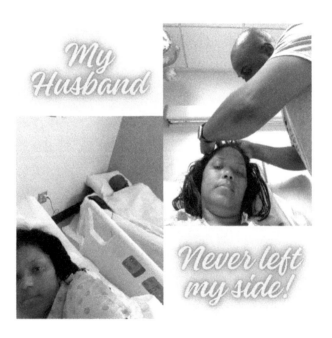

My mom joked with Ben about how he was so intentional about getting to me during this time. She too praised God for him and how he cared for me when I needed it the most. She also spent time caring for me while at the hospital, watching, praying, and making sure I was good.

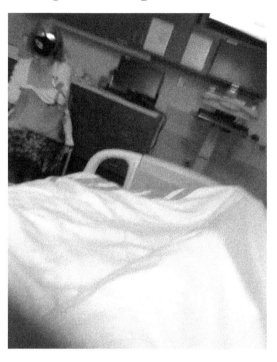

Every day, I journaled letters to Jesus expressing my appreciation, gratitude, love for sparing my life, and my family's heart from grief. I also journaled the events that transpired, how I was feeling about it all, and how I was feeling in my body and mind. I knew things could be much different. I could have been gone in that moment and they could have been planning my homegoing, *but God*! Thank God for saying, NO! I shall live and not die!

Staying in the Moment: I wrote in my journal on 9/28/2020 "Father you are good, and I am having trouble expressing how I feel about the favor, grace, mercy, goodness you have shown to me. Thank you for loving me, fighting for me, thank you for being sovereign in my life! To You be all the Glory and Honor! Placed for your Glory! Love, Sonya"

Moment of Reflection: Write a moment you had trouble expressing your feelings of unmerited favor and benefits of God.

_____

_____

_____

_____

_____

_____

_____

_____

_____

_____

_____

_____

_____

_____

_____

_____

_____

_____

_____

Moment 7

Encourage yourself!

10/5/2020 I wrote God's word in my journal, proclaiming and rejoicing in Him:

I will say of the Lord!!

O give thanks unto the Lord for He is good!
Greater is He that is in me than he that is in the world!

No weapon formed against me shall prosper!

Great is the Lord and greatly to be praised!
Jesus loves me this I know!
Oh magnify the Lord with me for He is worthy to be praise!

Jesus loves me this I know!

Oh, magnify the Lord for He is worthy to be praise!
God is a good God a good, good Father!

I will call upon the Lord who is worthy to be praised!
God is my refuge and strength a very present help in trouble!
There is power in the name of Jesus!

None like the Lord!

He is Lord, all powerful, all knowing, sovereign, worthy, great, mighty, compassionate, loving!

I shall live and not die!

Psalm 91 (KJV) With Long Life will I Satisfy Him!!

"He that dwelleth in the secret place of the most High shall abide under the shadow of the Almighty.

I will say of the LORD, He is my refuge and my fortress: my God; in him will I trust.

Surely he shall deliver thee from the snare of the fowler, and from the noisome pestilence.

He shall cover thee with his feathers, and under his wings shalt thou trust: his truth shall be thy shield and buckler.

Thou shalt not be afraid for the terror by night; nor for the arrow that flieth by day;

Nor for the pestilence that walketh in darkness; nor for the destruction that wasteth at noonday.

A thousand shall fall at thy side, and ten thousand at thy right hand; but it shall not come nigh thee.

Only with thine eyes shalt thou behold and see the reward of the wicked.

Because thou hast made the LORD, which is my refuge, even the most High, thy habitation;

There shall no evil befall thee, neither shall any plague come nigh thy dwelling.

For he shall give his angels charge over thee, to keep thee in all thy ways.

They shall bear thee up in their hands, lest thou dash thy foot against a stone.

Thou shalt tread upon the lion and adder: the young lion and the dragon shalt thou trample under feet.

Because he hath set his love upon me, therefore will I deliver him: I will set him on high, because he hath known my name.

He shall call upon me, and I will answer him: I will be with him in trouble; I will deliver him, and honour him.

With long life will I satisfy him, and shew him my salvation.

Amen!! I will say of the LORD!!"

Staying in the Moment: God did it for me! He didn't have to do it, but He did! Oh, how I Love Jesus! A new thing He did, God did, so I will do! No goodness of my own! Higher in Jesus, Placed for His Glory!

Moment of Reflection: Take a moment to encourage yourself in the Lord. Write your encouragement below.

_____

_____

_____

_____

_____

_____

_____

_____

_____

_____

_____

_____

_____

_____

_____

_____

_____

_____

_____

_____

Moment 8

After 14 days in the hospital, I was scheduled to be released. Oh, the joy I felt as I prepared to go home to my family, to my bed, to my bathroom. ☺ With all that I had endured, experienced, and overcome, I was grateful to my God for bringing me through. I was rolled into that hospital on my back, but my good, good Father allowed me to WALK out of that hospital without the assistance of anyone or thing. Like I literally got up, got dressed, and the nurse said they are waiting on a wheelchair, and I responded, "Oh I don't need a wheelchair I am ready. Can I just walk down?" She agreed and made sure I was ok. My husband had gone down to bring the car around and I walked out of those hospital doors up to the car and got in! The tears of joy, gratitude, and the praise that was sent up, to God be the Glory! Won't he do it!? Yes, HE will! For I know this didn't have to be, according to many this shouldn't have been, But God!!

The first stop was to visit my grandbabies, I missed them so much. Again, as we pulled up in the driveway and I saw the smiles from my family, tears began to flow once again. We were all so thankful to see each other and be able to embrace, and witness what the Lord had done.

The next stop would be home sweet home! As we approached the driveway, I was in shock and here we went again, tears! My mother-in-law had placed red ballons down the driveway and on my yard chair that I would often spend time in daily. I felt so blessed to have made it back home and to be able to feel, touch, and smell every part of the experience. I got out of the car, raised my hands in praise, walked over to my chair, and sat outside for a moment and took it all in!

Staying in the Moment: God did it for me! He didn't have to do it, but He did! Oh, how I Love Jesus! The tears, the red ballons, the embraces they all weren't in remembrance of me but a celebration of me being OK, alive and well and a sentiment to God for His healing, deliverance, covering and goodness!

Moment of Reflection: Thank God for the people in your life that is truly God sent and there for you! List them and say a prayer for them.

_____
_____
_____
_____
_____
_____
_____
_____
_____
_____
_____
_____
_____
_____
_____
_____
_____
_____

Moment 9

Placed for His Glory!

Oh God, I thank you for this testimony. Knowing that I am placed for His Glory. No matter what obstacles I have faced, I am placed for His Glory! I am placed, positioned, and assigned for His Glory. Because even though I went through, the place that I was in, He didn't let me stay there. He allowed me to be placed in it and brought out of it for His glory. I am a living example of Isaiah 43 1-7. So, glory be to God that my portion does not result in the short end of the stick. I did not die as a result of the brain aneurysm. I do not have any disabilities physically or mentally as a result of the brain aneurysm. I did not succumb to what could have been. I was rolled in the hospital but walked out! I am here today able to walk, talk, run, praise, work, drive, eat, drink, and give God all the Glory for His goodness. I know my portion was the pathway to something Greater!!! Thank you, Jesus! God knows my name and His love for me is like no other!!! As I write, I am in tears, tears of so much joy and gratefulness to my Savior. It didn't have to be, but God said it is so! You shall live and not die to declare my goodness.

But God

Isaiah 43:1-7

But now, this is what the LORD says—
he who created you, Jacob,
he who formed you, Israel:
"Do not fear, for I have redeemed you;
I have summoned you by name; you are mine.
² When you pass through the waters,
I will be with you;
and when you pass through the rivers,
they will not sweep over you.
When you walk through the fire,
you will not be burned;
the flames will not set you ablaze.
³ For I am the LORD your God,
the Holy One of Israel, your Savior;
I give Egypt for your ransom,
Cush[a] and Seba in your stead.
⁴ Since you are precious and honored in my sight,
and because I love you,
I will give people in exchange for you,
nations in exchange for your life.
⁵ Do not be afraid, for I am with you;
I will bring your children from the east
and gather you from the west.
⁶ I will say to the north, 'Give them up!'
and to the south, 'Do not hold them back.'
Bring my sons from afar
and my daughters from the ends of the earth—
⁷ everyone who is called by my name,

whom I created for my glory,
whom I formed and made."

The Sovereignty of God…

A very vital and pivotal phase of this journey for me, was dealing with something I had not dealt with or felt before. I was interacting with many and sharing the goodness of the Lord which seemed like almost every day, at every opportunity. All the while I was grateful, rejoicing, healthy, humbled and feasting on the goodness of the Lord. I was experiencing something I have never experienced before, nor did I know it was considered to be a real thing. I tried to explain to my husband how I was feeling but could not really put it into words that made sense because I did not quite understand it myself in many ways.

I would share my story knowing that many did not have the outcome or experience I had. They lost their loved ones to a brain aneurysm, or their loved ones are disable as a result of their brain aneurysm. So, as I would share or see someone that I knew had a story, I would feel a certain feeling that at the sight of me would bring pain to them with thoughts of their loss but my survival. Then one day, I mentioned to my daughter how I was feeling, and she said to me, "Mom that's called "Survivor's guilt."

I was like, "What???" And she began to explain that she learned this in college while studying nursing. She began to share with me what it meant. Survivor's guilt is defined as a particular kind of guilt that develops in people who have survived a life-threatening situation. Some survivors feel guilty that they survived when others died. Survivor's guilt is also common in those who have survived medical traumas. In my instance, having lived through the survival of a brain aneurysm I was having feelings of guilt related to my own survival while others I knew of personally and not personal but heard about, died.

It absolutely blew my mind to finally be able to put into context what I was feeling. I felt better to be able to discover what I was feeling psychologically, *But God*! God gave me peace and grace to move forward, owning the miracle that was wrought in my life without the guilt! God gave me a word that it's a privilege to be a walking miracle.

So, as I made my way back out and about in my community, like trips to the grocery store, pharmacy, I felt blessed and overwhelmed with joy from the Lord. I felt privileged to carry the evident hand of God on my life. Everyone that heard about the brain aneurysm and my survival, that I encountered, and I do mean everyone, no matter where or what we were in the middle of, we stopped and gave God the glory. The look on the faces was as if they'd seen a ghost, or complete shock I would say. To see me up walking, talking, functioning was a present-time miracle to witness, and it showed on each face and was heard in the conversations exchanged. Every outing turned into a conversation of praise and sharing of my testimony. God got and still gets ALL the glory! I still today share the goodness of God for His glory! It was beautiful. I am so grateful to be used by God to be considered His servant in honoring Him and giving Him His glory to be a light in the world! Yes, it was a miracle. I am a miracle and will always remember the sovereignty of God in my life! He can do what He wants, how He wants, for who He wants, when He wants. He doesn't need permission; He is God all by Himself! Oh God, I thank you!

Moment of Reflection: Read Isaiah 43:1-7 again. Write down what comes up for you as you read.

_____

_____

_____

_____

_____

_____

_____

_____

_____

_____

_____

_____

_____

_____

_____

_____

_____

_____

_____

Moment 10

No Cliché…

My PORTION does not result in the short end of the stick; it is the PATHWAY to something GREATER! We often say things, repeatedly. We hear things, repeatedly. Somethings become a cliché, a phase or opinion that is overused and betrays a lack of original thought. The short end of the stick is one of those phrases. This expression means to receive worse than others, unfair, unfavorable treatment. When the Lord gave me this theme for my iCare iShare with Sonya and Friends segment, I had no idea it would become so significant and personal and in the manner that it did. But oh God it did, and it resonated with power during and after my experience. It was no cliché it was real, and it was the pathway to something Greater!

When God gives you a word, believe it with all your heart that it is working for your good and that there is nothing cliché about the word of God. In His word stands power, healing, restoration, deliverance and freedom!

Women Of God on the Frontline victorious through Prayer, Faith, Courage, Worship and Power is the title of my very first book. I published this book in 2019. This book was birthed by God and has been a blessing to me and many. This book helps to lead, encourage, and inspire women of God all over the world. It is a devotional that prepares women of God when God places you on the frontline. With insights about Esther, a woman who is proof God can use the less likely to do great exploits. In this book, I am led to fuel the heart, mind, and spirit with tactical tools to keep you strong and courageous.

Purpose, purpose, purpose! God is the greatest architect! When I wrote this book, I had no idea it would have such an impact on my life in the way in which it would. While in the hospital those 14 days, I revisited my written words, and it blessed me all over again. I went through each of those five, what I called in my book, "tactical tools" of prayer, faith, courage, worship and power while on the frontline.

A heart synced with God's in prayer is vital and makes a difference. Biblical faith is applying scriptures appropriately. God, in turn, gives us the courage to leave the outcome in His hands because you can't manipulate the results in your favor. And the power and presence of God grants you His ability to achieve the impossible through Him. Above all, worship the Lord with our whole heart, and passion for Christ.

Staying in the Moment: We owe it to ourselves to walk in victory despite our circumstances. We as Women of God face many challenges. However, we are more than conquerors; we are survivors. Know that what we go through does not decide what God can do in and through you.

Moment of Reflection:

1) There is a preparation time: As we experience God's preparation time, it may feel the journey is long and eventful. However, the refining of our character is essential to God's plan for our life. God cannot use a proud woman.

2) God's Favor is important: I obtained favor of the Lord. When you live a life pleasing to God, by obeying His will you will gain favor with Him, resulting in favor with people as well.

3) God works in His own time and season: Don't leap into the calling on your life without preparation but wait for God's timing and alignment. God will move in His time when we stay faithful and alert to His leadings.

4) With God, our circumstances do not hinder our future: My circumstance does not decide what God can do in and through, my faith does!

Moment 11

Greatest Turnaround…

We do not always get to see the who, what, when, where's or loose ends, but that does not mean things are not coming together for our good. That morning as we experienced what felt like would be a possible loss, God was planning the most remarkable turnaround. Oh yes! What was meant for our bad, God turned it around for our good! God's hand of divine intervention was moving to set things right, to tie up the loose ends before the story even began. *"It is the Lord who goes before you. He will be with you. He will not leave you or forsake you. Do not fear or be dismayed."* **(Deuteronomy 31:8)**

I witnessed it working out by looking at the turnarounds:

1. My husband worked a shift that day that allowed him to be home and in bed with me.
   a. For over 24 years my husband has worked a schedule where his shift changes every week. Every week he is on a different shift. He could

have very easily worked what is called his 11-7 shift, where he would've been at work the moment I got sick and would have come home later to possibly find me in a worse state or even worse... gone. *But God!*

2. He is a heavy sleeper, and had worked 12 hours, yet this time he was awoken by me making an abnormal noise.

    a. My husband can sleep through anything. When his head hits the pillow, he is out, especially when he has worked over 8 hours. This particular week, he worked 12 hours, multiple days in a row. So, for him to hear what sounded like a strange noise coming from me was all God. I can make noise intentionally and he does not hear me. *But God!*

3. My daughter decided to return home for a short while following her graduating from college. This decision allowed her to be home for such a time as this!

    a. Shyia had been gone for three and a half years away in college and the younger boys were at home with me and Dad. 9 months prior to me becoming sick, this shifted. The boys were away at college and our daughter was at home. She was such a key part of this journey. Her sincere prayers, support, and care I'll cherish to eternity. She stepped up in more ways than one, in every area that was needed. I'm forever grateful for her! She could have decided to leave home after graduation however, she was at home for such a time as this. But God!

4. God allowed me enough strength to voice where I wanted to be taken for medical attention resulting in me not having to be taken to a facility that would not have been prepared for my care.

   a. I could have been in a medical state where I had no choice but to go by ambulance to our local county hospital. God was in the details, allowed my vitals to be strong in spite of, and gave my husband direction to take me by car to a hospital outside our county where I would receive the care God had waiting for me. They took me in immediately, began working on me, and found the problem right away. They ordered my transfer to MUSC for further treatment and diagnosis. Had I gone to my local institution the necessary treatment and referrals and timing of it all would not have been available to me. *But God!*

5. The best neurologist was on call the very morning I had a need, and he was assigned to me.

   a. As I was leaving Roper being transferred to MUSC, the doctors were speaking to my husband and sister about what to expect upon arrival. He said that I would be cared for by Dr. Lena, and that if I wanted any Neurologist to care for me it would be Dr. Lena. He is the best, and he was on call, and would be prepping for my arrival. *But God!*

Fast forward, it's now 3 years and 5 months later. I am still here in Jesus' name. I've had 2 additional surgeries for the aneurysm with the final one being January 2023. I had my final angiogram appointment June 2023. I was cleared and released. I survived what the devil wanted to kill me! God turned it!

God is my creator and sustainer. God is holy and just. God is loving and kind. I won't ever forget what He did for me! God took care of me! God fought for me! God was not against me, He was with me, working for me, through me, and fighting for me. I praise God for He has never lost a battle and He never wastes a battle! I am humbled, grateful, and overwhelmed with his endless love for me! Jesus I'll never forget! I am placed for His glory. My life will always be my testimony. My story for His glory!

All these turnarounds point us to the greatest U-turn of all: Christ came to undo the fall. He took Adam's disaster, our disasters, and in a most unforeseen way, He conquered death and gave us life.

Have you had any situations where you thought all hope was lost only to encounter the very hand of God that would come in and turn things around just like that? Well, you just found out it was our good Father that was all up and in it! Have you ever wondered how it will all work out? I will tell you; We Win!

"I had fainted, unless I had believed to see the goodness of the Lord in the land of the living." **-Psalms 27:13**

I encourage you to not back down from the enemy. If or when God places you for His glory, move forward in prayer, faith, courage, worship, and God's power breaking every chain.

Let's strengthen our prayer life which is our relationship with God. We're to grow in faith, which is our reaction to His truth. Be courageous knowing God is in control of the outcome. And worship Him for who He is, knowing that everything around you may change day to day, but our God never changes, and neither should our worship. And last, but not least declare the never-failing power of God which is His anointing and presence in your life that will ultimately breach every chain.

Remember always to acknowledge *But God* moments, that no matter the circumstances your life is your testimony that you are placed for His Glory!

About the Author!

Lady Sonya Michelle Snell is the visionary and founder of Women of God on the Frontline; a ministry birthed by God to serve, encourage, and empower women all over. Has a heart for women, which drives her passion to empower and encourage! She gives all praise to her Lord and Savior Jesus Christ for his strength, love for her, and faithfulness to her! She is humbled to be used by God and forever grateful to have been gifted with the audacity to be unique! Her motto: Jesus is the difference that makes the difference in me!

To connect with Lady Sonya, you may email her at:

wogotfl@gmail.com

Or follow her on social media:

Facebook- Women of God on the Frontline

Instagram- @womenofgodonthefrontline

Printed in the USA
CPSIA information can be obtained
at www.ICGtesting.com
CBHW061523150324
5431CB00013B/187